cloverleaf books™

Nature's Patterns

Do Trees Get Hungry?

Noticing Plant and Animal Traits

Martha E. H. Rustad

illustrated by Mike Moran

M MILLBROOK PRESS · MINNEAPOLIS

For Luke and Samantha,
from Auntie Martha
—M.E.H.R.

For Keira —M.M.

Millbrook Press
A division of Lerner Publishing Group, Inc.
241 First Avenue North
Minneapolis, MN 55401 USA

For reading levels and more information, look up this title at
www.lernerbooks.com.

Main body text set in Slappy Inline 18/28.
Typeface provided by T26.

Library of Congress Cataloging-in-Publication Data

The Cataloging-in-Publication Data for Do Trees Get Hungry?:
Noticing Plant and Animal Traits is on file at the Library of
Congress.
ISBN 978-1-4677-8559-4 (lib. bdg.)
ISBN 978-1-4677-8605-8 (pbk.)
ISBN 978-1-4677-8606-5 (EB pdf)

Manufactured in the United States of America
1 – BP – 7/15/15

TABLE OF CONTENTS

Chapter One

Our Class Pet

Meet our friend Jojo! She is a gecko. Jojo lives in her tank in our classroom. We all help take care of her.

Mr. Andre asks, "Whose turn is it to feed Jojo?" He checks the job chart.

Taye feeds Jojo mealworms. Attly gives her fresh water.

We take turns holding her carefully.

We love our pet!

Geckos are reptiles. Reptiles breathe air, have a backbone and scaly skin, and are cold-blooded. That means their bodies are the same temperature as their surroundings. Most reptiles hatch from eggs.

Today we're leaving Jojo in our classroom. We are going on a nature hike! Our teacher says we are going to learn about **patterns in nature.**

Demarco says, "Aren't patterns part of math class?"

"Well, a pattern is anything that happens over and over," Mr. Andre says.

"Like how we have hot dogs at lunch every Friday!" says Mae.

Mr. Andre asks us to observe nature. He says that means we should **look around and watch carefully.**

We walk to a nearby park. Attly sees a robin!
"I wish Jojo could have come along," she says. "I bet she has never seen a bird."

Mr. Andre asks, "Can you think of ways that Jojo and a robin are alike?"

Keisha points out, "Jojo eats worms. Robins do too."

"That's a pattern," our teacher says. "**Animals need food.** How else is Jojo like other animals?"

Hans says, "She drinks water. So does my dog!"

Asif says, "She needs a safe place to live. Like birds need nests."

We found more patterns!
Animals need water and homes.

Chapter Two

Plant Patterns

Next, we walk toward the woods. Mae sees a flower!

Mr. Andre asks us to think about plants. "How is this daisy like an animal?"

Li laughs. "It's not!" she says.

"Well, animals need water," Attly says. "Plants need water too. **Another pattern!**"

Mr. Andre asks, "**What happens when plants don't get enough water?**"

"They get thirsty?" Keisha guesses.

"Yeah, they dry up and die," answers Taye.

Plants soak up water through roots in the ground.

Demarco asks, "Do trees get hungry?"
"Not really," our teacher responds and smiles.
"Who remembers how plants get food?"

Li raises her hand. **"Plants get food from the sun!"** she says.

"Correct!" Mr. Andre says. "Sunlight, along with water and air, helps plants make their food."

We talk about how plants and animals both need food. But their food is very different.

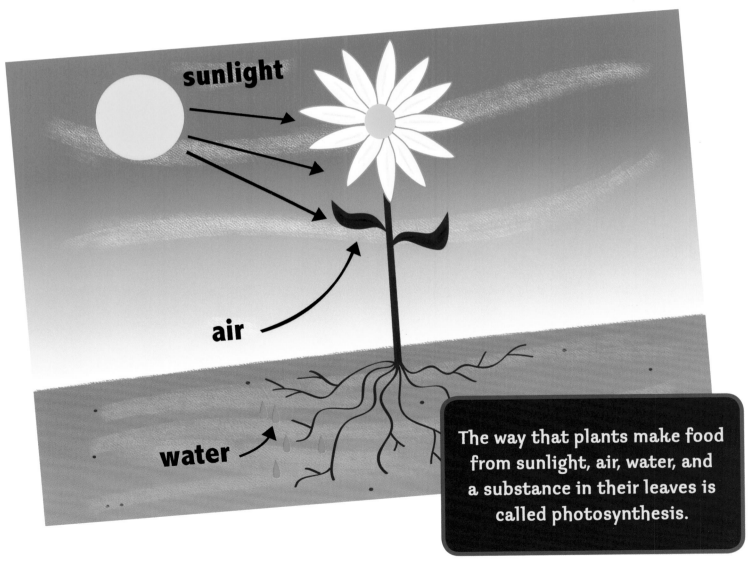

sunlight

air

water

The way that plants make food from sunlight, air, water, and a substance in their leaves is called photosynthesis.

Mr. Andre asks us to look carefully at the leaves on an oak tree.

We notice that all the leaves on one tree are the same shape.

Hans says, "But some leaves are big. And some are small."

Attly points out a birch tree. "Those leaves are a very different shape!" Attly says.

"Good job looking closely," our teacher says. **"Different kinds of trees have differently shaped leaves."**

We gather a few leaves to take back and show Jojo.

Needles on pine trees are another kind of leaf.

Chapter Three

Animal Patterns

"**Look!**" Asif exclaims. We see a tiny squirrel running behind a bigger squirrel.

"It must be a mama and baby," Li says. Our teacher asks if we've seen other baby animals.

Some baby animals look very different from their parents. Tadpoles look like fish, but they grow up to be frogs.

Keisha says, "My cat had kittens. The babies looked like **little cats!** But their fur was all different."

"Jojo!" Taye says. "She was so small at first. Then she grew bigger."

We notice that baby animals look mostly like adult animals. Same look, different size. **Another pattern!**

Hans finds a colorful piece of bird eggshell on the ground.

"Didn't Jojo hatch from an egg?" Attly asks.

"Could that be a pattern too?" Taye says.

Our teacher agrees. Birds and most reptiles both hatch from eggs.

Asif says, "Eggs are small. And plants grow from small seeds."

"Another pattern!" says Mae. "Little eggs and seeds grow into bigger animals and plants!"

Mr. Andre says, "You all are amazing pattern finders!"

Chapter Four

Patterns in Nature

Back in our classroom, Asif shows Jojo the leaves we gathered.

"Did you miss us, Jojo?" Li asks. Our gecko blinks.

Our teacher asks if we learned anything new on our walk.

Keisha raises her hand. "Plants and animals are so much alike!"

"Plants need water, and so do animals!" Demarco says. We talk about the patterns we saw.

Ring! School is done. Mr. Andre asks us to make sure Jojo has clean water before we leave. Jojo takes a drink as we say, "See you tomorrow!"

Nature Treasure Hunt

Be a nature watcher! Look for these plant and animal traits. See if you can find your own patterns.

You will need:
a notebook
a pencil or pen

1) Make a chart like this:

Plant or Animal	Where	Appearance	Activity

2) Find a safe place to watch nature. For example, look out a window in your home or when you are in a car or bus. Or go to a park or on a nature walk with an adult.

3) Watch for animals and plants. Look for birds, squirrels, or other wildlife. Find trees, vines, or other plants.

4) Write down where you see a plant or an animal. Is it in the sky or on the ground?

5) Note how it looks. What color is it? Is it bigger than you or smaller than you?

6) Write what it is doing. Is the plant growing in the shade? Is the squirrel running up a tree?

7) Look for patterns in your observations. For example, do you see any birds and flowers that are the same color? What other patterns do you see?

GLOSSARY

bird: an animal that has feathers on all or most of its body. Birds breathe air, have a backbone, are born from eggs, and are warm-blooded (they make their own body heat).

egg: a round object laid by a female animal. Young animals hatch from eggs.

gecko: a type of small lizard

observe: to look closely

pattern: something that is repeated again and again

photosynthesis: the way that plants make food for themselves using sunlight, water, air, and a substance in their leaves called chlorophyll

reptile: an animal that has dry, scaly skin and breathes air. Reptiles have a backbone and are cold-blooded (their bodies are the same temperature as their surroundings). Most reptiles hatch from eggs.

root: a plant part that grows down into the ground and soaks up water and nutrients

seed: a tiny plant part that when covered in soil grows and becomes a new plant

BOOKS

Lawrence, Ellen. *Cooking with Sunshine: How Plants Make Food.* New York: Bearport, 2013.
Read more about how plants make their own food.

Morgan, Sally. *Animal Life Cycles.* Mankato, MN: Smart Apple Media, 2012.
Learn more about patterns in animal life cycles.

Salas, Laura Purdie. *A Leaf Can Be . . .* Minneapolis: Millbrook Press, 2012.
Find out about the many roles leaves play, from shade spiller to mouth filler, in this poetic exploration of leaves throughout the year.

Sawyer, J. Clark. *Patterns in the Park. Seeing Patterns All Around.*
New York: Bearport, 2015.
Head out to a park to look for lines, swirls, and other patterns.

WEBSITES

Animal Homes
http://www.kidport.com/reflib/science/animalhomes/animalhomes.htm
Find out more about different animal homes.

Sid the Science Kid: Vegetable Patterns
http://pbskids.org/sid/fablab_vegetablepatterns.html
Play a game to make a pattern of vegetables.

LERNER e SOURCE™
Expand learning beyond the printed book. Download free, complementary educational resources for this book from our website, www.lernerresource.com.